Winter White
and
Summer Gold

Available from A Tribe of Two Press:

Three Learning Stories by
Paula Underwood:

Who Speaks for Wolf
Winter White and Summer Gold
Many Circles, Many Paths

And to be used with them:
Three Strands in the Braid:
A Guide for Enablers of Learning

————

The Audio Tape
Three Strands in the Braid
Paula Underwood tells the three stories
with original music and Wolf Song

————

Who Speaks for Wolf
Fully illustrated with original
art by Frank Howell

————

The Walking People:
A Native American Oral History

————

For more information contact
A Tribe of Two Press
PO Box 913 • Georgetown TX   78627 • 512 / 930-5576

Winter White and Summer Gold

A Native American Learning Story

by
Paula Underwood

Cover art by Frank Howell

A Tribe of Two Press • San Anselmo, California • 1994

Cover art by Frank Howell
from the original Illustrated edition of
Who Speaks for Wolf

Produced by AMS Publications
Georgetown, Texas

Library of Congress Catalog Card #94-078238
ISBN # 1-879678-09-8

A Tribe of Two Press
PO Box 913
Georgetown, TX 78627
(512) 930-5576

Three Native American Learning Stories

My Ancestors, for more than 10,000 years, taught themselves how the human system functions - - from sensitivity to decision. In so doing, they began to see how it was that Many Paths to Understanding were requisite - - some more easily open to This One or That, some so closed that the need for alternate paths became excruciatingly clear.

They saw also how these various paths must be woven together into a whole - - so that the Whole People may prosper.

For that reason, they slowly crafted over many, many centuries complementary learning paths which - - when woven together - - gave memory and access - - wholeness and utility.

As a bridge toward understanding, as a way of practicing life without falling over its cliffs, as a way of honing a keen appreciation of the possibilities and of the wholeness within which those possibilities may be identified . . . the People evolved Three Learning Stories . . . One for each fundamental aspect of this Life Experience . .

One for Body . .

One for Mind . .

One for Spirit . .

Each of these stories is based on an historic circumstance. Each is modified and enhanced to encourage, to create a space in which new learning may occur. Used again and again down through the centuries, they enable each to develop the skills necessary to use Life Experience effectively.

In this way, they function like an access code to the data base that any gathered experience affords. They are like simple-yet-complex piano exercises that enable the later playing of great symphonies.

It is with great joy that we bring you these Three Learning Stories - - Three Strands in the Braid of Life.

Paula Underwood - 1994

Winter White
and
Summer Gold

All of the leaves
on all of the trees
were particularly soft that spring

New shoots of all the varying grasses
burst through the crusted, yielding earth
each small fissure forming a minute valley
out of which this new life sprung

Waters began the soft sounds of spring
Winter White
melting into the clarity of fresh water
seeping through earth to thickening roots
gathering into cascades
renewing their long trek to the sea

There was joy
Among the People
Earth began a new song
and the People
voiced her melody

Those who had been restrained
by the deepening snow
sought the freedom this new warmth afforded

Steeped in the exuberance of unrestrained motion
some of the people
already found their way to that part of Earth
which would yield Summer's gift
exploring last year's clearing
seeking with probing sticks
the nature of the soil
soon to receive
the gathered future of the People

Some other of the People
    were already among the trees
        slowly convincing them to make way
            for our Three Sacred Sisters
For after this Spring comes another . . .
        and, after that, a third

And surely
    only those Peoples
        who understand the sequence of Summers - -
            encouraging trees toward corn - -
                gift Earth's children with our Summer Gold

New waters swelled in every stream
    cracking and carrying off winter's icy coat
Almost with the sound of the first crack
    small boys appeared at each stream edge
        sharpened stick lances poised
            in search of slow moving fish
        eager to find them
            before their winter sluggishness
                washed away with the spring waters

Soon
>*the stream-side trees were festooned with nets*
>>*rapidly filling with the sudden fruit*
>>>*of these same spears*

Each valiant hunter
>*maintained his silent concentration*

Yet
>*when any net filled and was taken down*
>>*cries echoed through the forest*
>>>*as the swollen nets made their way*
>>>>*from stream to prepared earth*

"Hoy Hoy - -
>*Look this way"*
>>*- - a young voice cries - -*
"Ya-a-ah Hoy - -
>*Spirit listens"*
>>*- -comes the answer - -*

And the trees at the edge of forest clearings
*   rapidly acquired the look of stream-side trees*
The pungence of fish too far from water
*   increasingly filled the forest air*

Now
    the women had come to the clearings
        singing songs of earth and warming air
        songs of thanks, also,
            for the netted fish . .
            for the life they would bring
                to the quickening corn

They sang:

    "From Earth the water comes

    "From waters the finned swimmers come
        Gathered in nets
        Swimming in that way through air
        They swim now through earth
        And accompany our Sacred Sisters

    "May each green stalk
        Rooted in earth and water
        Remember the gift of fish"

Somewhere beyond the hill
men searched the earth
for indications of life

This early in the warming of Earth
only certain of our Brothers were sought - -
their four-footed marks
showing us their direction

Like certain fish
many others were neither sought nor found - -
their participation in the Great Earth Dance
in the beginning of new life
being preferable to the People

No one
	concerned themselves with the houses

During the deep snow
	all of the customary renewal was undertaken
		clothing mended or begun
		panels within the houses replaced
		worked bone and shell patterns
			set with careful stitches on ceremonial dress
		ancient patterns strung once more
			with fresh new thongs

Then later- -
	after the season of growth - -
		thoughts would turn to the houses themselves
		supports would be again secured
		thongs woven, wrapped, and wet with stream water
			would shrink slowly under watchful eyes
				securing each joint against unexpected change
		bark panels would be placed against these joints

"Let the house be secure as a water carrier"
- - some of the men would sing - -

"As no water drips from a well-made basket
    Let no water drip through this well-made roof"

And
    there would be laughter as one told another
        that the heads in his family
            surely would be damp long before spring
                corn perhaps sprouting from someone's pocket
                    long before it sprouted from any earth

And with laughter
And with song
And with mutual admonitions
    to take greater care
        this task, too
            would be well accomplished

But now
*   the houses stood empty of their inhabitants*
*   Neither side of the walls*
*   received any patient attention*

The world outside was stirring

Last winter was difficult

A winter of too much snow
  followed a summer of too little rain

Little kernels of future life
  had been carefully stored
    preserved as one preserves the future
      of a Whole People

During the winter
  no one asked for this corn

  Not one cry was heard
    even from the smallest of the People

  Each morning began with a song
    from She Who Adjudicated within each Long House

"Great One, we give thanks
  For the bounty of Earth
  For her kindness to us

"Great One, we give thanks
  For the wisdom of the People
    Who preserve the seed of Future Life

"Great One, we give thanks
  There is little . . .
    But there is enough"

Quiet murmurs were heard among the People
  gentle echoes of purposefulness
    and then . . .

"Snow Soup!"
  - - someone called - -

And laughter drowned the footsteps
   of those who were young
      as they danced out through the door
         to gather fresh snow
      filling each water carrier with snow to be heated
         for of wood there was truly enough

While the Snow Gatherers fulfilled their purpose
    many women counted again
        the carefully preserved bounty
            of last summer's drying earth
        dividing each kind
            into the same number of portions
                as there were days left until spring
                    and people left who were hungry

Each Snow Gatherer
    received a portion of berry cake, however small
        as a gift for this gift of fresh snow
    According to each individual nature
        they would swallow quickly . . .
    or munch slowly . . .
    or save for later in the day
        enjoying the knowledge of this tasteful wealth
            to be consumed at will

But surely
    each one ate or drank or saved and later enjoyed
        this usual beginning to each day
            understanding the sore mouth sickness
                that might otherwise come
                wishing health for themselves and others

Later in the day
    one or more of the Three Sacred Sisters
        greeted them from the cooking pots - -
            Corn or Beans, sometimes Squash
Even with such limited stores
    the women in each Long House
        managed variety in every meal

The favorite winter places to dig under the snow
    for fresh roots and occasional leaves
        were carefully husbanded
        portioned slowly through the winter as a reminder
            that Spring, after all, would come
And dried herbs, those memories of Spring
    were kept through the winter
        varying the flavor of every dish

This was the time
　for the smaller boys whose lighter weight
　　might not break through this crust of snow

They set snares
　for an occasional squirrel
Dug tunnels
　from one house to another
Searched under trees
　for nests of sleeping furred creatures

These small gifts of fur and food
　were appreciated by all

"We will feast"
　- - the women cried - -
　　carefully cutting each portion
　　　into the simmering pot
　　sharing even the smallest such gift equally
　　　with all the people within that Long House

And
    songs would be sung to the brave hunter
      who had attained, perhaps, his seventh winter
        along with one more squirrel

Sometimes
    one such hunter might not return

    His path would be sought
      by those taller than the snow
    And carefully built tunnels would disappear
      beneath the flailing feet
        of those who hunted the hunter

Found at last
    on the other side of a collapsed tunnel
      he would ride home
        on shoulders glad at the weight
        protesting all the while the destruction
        of too many snow passages

The young girls
   disappeared with equal frequency
      down such snowy passages
         seeking the company of others
         seeking their own first winter digging places

      Even grass roots might be welcome
         in a winter which left the People leaner
            as the days progressed

Happy songs
   were sung to any such
      who returned
         with food for the simmering pots

      "Here is one who understands
         The needs of the people around her

      "Unbidden, she seeks winter's cold
         And returns with memories of Spring

       "We feast . . .
         We feast . . .
           We feast"

And so the winter passed - -

Sometimes
    the women would decide to ask a small band of men
        to search the woods for a larger one
            among our four-footed brothers
                who might join our Three Sisters
                    dancing with them in the cooking pot

But in such a winter - -
    with such snow and wind - -
        they would see how easy it was
            for fewer to return than those who left

    Understanding this
        it would seem to them that a lonely stomach
            is preferable to a lonely heart
And
    they would speak against such missions

And yet
  the men - - seeing the thinning faces - -
    would go out from time to time
      searching the whitened woods
      or sit cross-legged on a frozen stream
        searching through the ice
          for those finned swimmers
            still moving through the blue-black waters

  In the shallower streams
    ice was cut and melted
      yielding not only water for washing
        but a finned swimmer here and there - -
          frozen in ice

And again
  Whatever came home in the hands of the hunter
    however small, however large
      was greeted with the same joy
        equally apportioned among all the fires
          within that large and loving home

Cries of
   "We feast . . .
      We feast . . .
         We feast"
beat against the soft panels
   that divided the rooms one from another
      and echoed against the walls

"Let the cold and dark
   remain outside"
      - - the echoes seemed to say - -

"Let the warmth and joy of family
   remain within"

And yet another thing occurred

During a scant winter
   no matter how small the gift
      from forest or from stream
   some portion
      was cut and hung in the smoke of the fire

"Here is Tomorrow"
   - - she who wielded the knife would cry - -

And
   all felt grateful
      to see this evidence of care - -
   this gift to the next day's need
      suspended before their eyes

"My eyes keep my stomach full"
   - - someone would laugh - -

"Were I as tall as you"
    - - some very young one might add - -

"My stomach, too, might seem full - -
    but my eyes
        are too distant from tomorrow's supper
            to fill my stomach"

It was said with dignity
    and the reply was equally quick

"To each in equal measure"
    - - one of the women would gently remonstrate - -

"More Snow Soup, quick"
    - - someone else would cry - -

And
    a young stomach
        none too happy with its contents
            would soon be at least full - -
                at least warm - -
        the next meal never too far off

"But if they were hungry, My Father, shouldn't they be fed?" I asked the one who sang this song.

"If they are fed more today and less tomorrow, where is the value?" he asked in return. "If their stomach grows larger with today's meal and even smaller with tomorrow's, will not their pain be greater?"

He paused, allowing me time to consider these alternatives, and then went on. "What, after all, is the purpose here?"

Through my mind flashed pictures of forest .. snow .. stream .. fire .. a Long House with people living together inside, surviving yet another winter. At last I saw the image.

"They are surviving," I replied. "All of them are surviving . . . every one. This is why the women do not encourage the men out in such difficult weather. A full stomach is not an equal trade for an empty space by the fire. Nor even . . ." I considered further, remembering all my father had said about cold and snow, chill winds and beating ice crystals. "Nor even the burning of the fingers caused by too much cold!"

A slight smile touched the corner of his mouth . . . blending slowly with the sharpened look of greater concentration. "Perhaps something else concerns you," he suggested.

I saw at once the puzzled frown that still divided my eyes, one from the other.

"Should they not, my Father, should they not give more to the children? Are they not the Future? Do not bones still grow and legs lengthen? Should they not have more of the offered food?"

"Consider what you have already learned," he replied.

And I considered, searched the forest with puzzled eyes, saw snares and tunnels, ice-sitting men and purposeful hunters. Nothing here answered my concern.

The bark-covered walls of the Owachira appeared before me, secure against the intrusion of snow, even snow mounting to the roof. I saw at last through these walls into the heart of the Long House, each family compartment set against the walls, partitions between them of woven saplings covered now with winter panels of soft worked skin. I saw the Central Fires down the center passage, wider than a hall, perhaps as wide as our living room. I saw Tomorrow hung in the smoke of each fire and felt hunger of my own, thinking those suspended strips of nourishment might find a happier home within my empty interior.

"Snow Soup, quick!" I heard someone cry . . . and the warming liquid cascaded down my throat, leaving a full but somehow unsatisfied stomach. With eager eyes I watched the women preparing the dancers for today's simmering pot.

"Not too long to wait," a voice next to me said. And I looked up, startled, at the hunter next to me. It was the man whose eyes filled his stomach. He was so tall he seemed to disappear into the ceiling. I saw at last the smile on his face — the same patient smile I saw so often beneath my father's questioning eyes.

I understood that love.

"Which of these women is my mother," I asked.

"They all are," he replied. And I understood him. For surely all the women in that Great House shared responsibility for each person within.

"No burden is too great," my father had said, "when many shoulders lift it."

But the Tall Hunter was speaking again. "If you have not yet chosen a mother," he said, "share mine," and he sat down beside me.

The freedom of each child to choose parents they might prefer raced through my mind, each step slowly taken, always in consultation with She Who Adjudicated within that Great House. For the first time I understood the implications.

"You see how it is," his hand swept out in indication. "This One is my mother, as I am her son. She will give to each of us from her simmering pot."

The woman ladled from basket to dish, handing the first dish . . . and then the second to her son. One of these he handed, in turn, to me.

I was on my knees in an instant, peering from his dish to mine. "They are the same," I said with no small astonishment. "But . . . but . . . you're so much *bigger* than I am!"

"Do you have an answer?" my father was asking.

The Long House disappeared around me. Mother of Hunter was already gone.

"Oh, don't go!" I cried out to the Hunter. But he smiled at me - - that same smile - - and was gone.

"I would be willing," the sadness in my voice lengthened to a sighing sound, "to have an empty stomach in order to live in such a house."

"I hear part of the answer, my Daughter. Now find the rest."

"He was bigger than me," I answered. "Much, much bigger. But his mother gave us each the same . . . exactly the same."

"Is that not in the manner of the People?" my father asked.

"But don't you see?" I asked with the untempered impatience of youth. "If he's so much bigger than I am, yet receives the same from one who is his mother more than mine . . . am I not given more?"

"You have the rest of your answer," my father smiled, "and more. For even those who count many, many winters and whose years weigh them down to a smaller stature, even these ones receive equal measure with the tallest hunter. It is the way we show respect for age. We have understood its value for a very long time."

Seeing no further questions in my eyes, my father settled back again and began the sonorous, rhythmic tones with which each Telling begins . . and recommences.

I have told you
  - - he intoned - -

  How it was for our people

Snow so deep
  that some mornings
    the long poles were necessary
      to clear the smoke holes in the roof

Snow so deep
  that after the storm
    the only incoming air
      filtered through that snow
  And once the smoke holes were cleared
    wall flaps were lifted
      revealing a second wall of snow

But

    snow sits in little bright crystals . . .
      and air passes easily through it . .
        unless by carelessness . .
          someone has allowed this access to air
            to thaw and then freeze again
  For I tell you now
    a wall of ice permits little transit of air

And so

  the women kept the center warm

But

    the compartments against the outside walls
      were kept cool to discourage thawing
  Even did some families move
    from this compartment . . and that one . .
      joining other families
      joining warmth with warmth

Then these uninhabited rooms were kept closed
    soft skin panels
        shielding such interiors
            from the warmth of fire
        securing access to air

And
    each such access was regularly checked
        to assure that no ice walls had yet formed
    Any such were dug away to soft, crystal snow
        with its gentle filtered air

For
    the well being of the People
        comes in many forms - -

That Which Is Consumed
    finds Two Paths
        toward energy and strength

The nature of Earth
   is filtered through her creatures
      toward the bubbling dance of each cooking pot
      toward each daily need

Even so
  is the nature of Sky
    the clear, ambient air
      filtered through snow crystals
        toward each Central Fire
      toward the rising and falling of breath
      toward each and every daily need

Such are the two paths

Now
    This same winter
        of snow tunnels and snares for squirrels,
        carefully husbanded food and Winter digging
        snow filtered air and smoke trails in the sky

    This same winter
        was a winter of such bitter cold
            that not even the line of Central Fires
                in each Long House seemed enough

Not even
    the Winter Robes prepared so lovingly
        by the women for their families
            from the gifts of Bear and Fox and Rabbit

Not even
    the covered walls around the People
        kept out the cold

Little hunting was possible

Even snares set for squirrel were rapidly buried
　　hidden by the new snow
And tunnels collapsed of this new weight
　　the intrusion of no Hunter's foot even necessary

This same winter
　　All the earth seemed frozen
　　　　In a long wait for spring

On the rare days when wind and snow allowed
　　few tracks were found
　　　　and even these few were rapidly lost

No new gift found its way
　　into the dancing waters of any bubbling pot

The women counted each mouthful of food
　　thinking now of the possibility
　　　　of a late spring and a hungry People

Now
  they told each other - -
    it is time for the sometimes food

And
  plans were laid
    for the gradual inclusion of foods
      that might otherwise not be eaten

Bark was peeled from many appropriate trees
  and the layer beneath carefully stripped away
    to slowly add to each cooking pot

"Share the Earth with me, my Brother"
  - - each gatherer explained to birch and elm - -

"I leave enough for you
  but without this gift
    there may be none of the People
      to dance beneath leaf-covered branches - -
      and think how much sorrow that would bring!"

Oaks were searched
    for any clinging acorn
A few crumbs of food
    were left here and there near snares
      for the smallest of the four-footeds
Even these were joyfully greeted
      and quickly shared by the cooking pots

But
    the seed corn was kept . .

And
    the promise of Tomorrow
      still hung over the fire . .

And
    berry cake was still enough to last
      - - day by day - -
        toward a possible spring

Now
    when I tell you this
      you will remember
        how each Long House is built . .
      out of poles and bark, furs and woven reeds
        and here it is
          that the People find last food

For
    when each attainable oak has been searched
    each bush deprived of its last winter berry
    each under-bark strip brought to the bubbling pot
      as a gift from forest to the People

Then
    do eyes turn to the nature of the House itself - -
      underbark is stripped from remaining poles
      some skins may be boiled
        for the last residue they contain
      reeds may be soaked
        and mashed into a digestible gruel

And
    although the People might design no feast
        along such lean-year lines
    During such years
        they are glad of even such resources
            and sing their inclusion
                into the dance of life hung over each Fire

My Father's voice grew still once more and my thoughts stretched out to encompass all he had said.

The bitterness of bark touched my thoughts . . and reeds pounded into a bread-like mass - - The unsatisfying warmth of Snow Soup filled my stomach once more - - touched, now, with the tang of boiled skins.

Providing for the future as they knew how to do, I understood each pot would contain the dance of a little corn, some roots, some beans - - reminders of the plenty that lay ahead. And now the persistent thuck, thuck of the pounders sounded within the House - - reminders of the patient care the women took of each and every person, encouraging the pith of bark and reed toward the possibility of digestion.

I saw how a People might sustain themselves past probable survival. Working together, each individual purpose sustaining the common goal, many feet followed a path that few alone might not survive.

I remembered the concern of others for my well being that somehow filled me along with the Snow Soup, and I saw how much farther a little will carry you when there is love in the House.

"It is the rest of the story," I said out loud. "The greatest flavoring for any food is love. The survival of the People requires love as well. It is the third step round the circle, the gift we add to Earth and Sky, the completion of our purpose."

"And no purpose beyond?" my Father asked.

I considered the nature of the circle the People danced . . . Earth and Sky and the Unity expressed as Love . . I saw the walls of the Great Long House, bubbling pots filled with dancing Sisters . . . or Snow Soup . . .

I saw . .

But I had never *seen* any such House! This image, which held for me all the clarity of constant association, I had built with the bark and poles of my father's words. Every corner I could look into - - and *know* what was there - - came from his patient answers to my many questions. It had been a long time . . a long time since any in my family had stepped within the structured walls of any Long House. And yet I saw the image, patiently transferred from generation to generation, as if I were my grandfather's grandmother.

"Why did you do it?" I asked .. and met my father's startled gaze. "Why did you listen and learn so patiently about something you never saw? Why do you sit with me now and explain until your legs no longer straighten when you stand?"

His startled gaze slowly softened into a smile.

"I was wondering," he answered at last, "what you have learned from this?"

And then I understood.

A way of life both he and I thought beautiful had been preserved. So clear in his mind and in mine that we could have built such a House, established such a People. No day passed but that we borrowed some Ancient Wisdom - - passed from generation to generation - - and understood more clearly our present circumstance.

"In our own way," I answered him, "we also sustain the People. We listen to the things they learned, thread them on the cords of our own thoughts, hold them close to the fire of our own vision, and suspend them at last in the smoke of our understanding .. preserving them for tomorrow.

"Through us, the People have survived more than the coldest Winter. Through us they have survived the centuries."

I was quiet for a long time, listening to the person I would become.   Listening to my own grandmother-voice which one day would speak so that others might learn.

At last my Father's words entered the silent space between us.

"I see understanding," he explained, "where before I saw only questions . . . I see learning." Again he waited until the inward turn of my thoughts gradually changed direction, becoming a willingness to listen.

As my eyes turned toward him, he began once more the rhythm of the chant, fingertips beating slowly . . against his folded knee.

I would be pleased to tell you
that our Brother, Bear, suddenly appeared
and offered himself to the People
But it was not so

I would be pleased even to tell you
that Beaver or Otter
walked up to the door of our Long House
to offer himself to the dancing waters
But neither was this so

The many last days of Winter
continued as they had begun
filled with Snow and Driving Wind
Sad, indeed
for any who sought new possibilities
for a dwindling store of food

And yet
    there was laughter in the House - -

One Hunter met another with the admonition
    "I thought you were a much larger man
        than you presently seem to be!"

    "Like Bear who sleeps all Winter"
        - - he replied - -
    "I need the warming sun of Spring
        to expand my shrunken Winter Self"

And
    all would laugh at the image of this man
        shrunk small with Winter cold
            suddenly expanding under a warming sun

    "Perhaps if you sit close enough to Fire . . ."
        - - some one suggested - -

And again . .
   rafters peeled bare of bark . .
      rang with the sound of merriment

   Even those working outside the House
      peeling back the last bark covering
         from its many poles
            maintained the pattern . . .
         stitching together one person and another
            through the mutuality of laughter

   "Tell me, my Brother"
      - - one of them asked - -

   "Will next Winter be a happier time than this?
      - - and he rubbed his stomach
         to make his concern even more evident

   "Look at it this way"
      - - his companion answered - -

"Perhaps next year
     we will think back over this Winter
          cooking pots filled with boiling bark
               the distance around each waist
                    growing smaller and smaller
and think . . .
          how lucky we were to have so much bark!
for surely
          next year there will be none left."

And
     he leapt down from the roof of that Long House
          the last of the bark clutched in his hand
          and ran through the House singing

". . . This year's plenty . . ."

And dropping an equal portion
     of the bark retrieved
          in each of the dancing waters
               suspended over the Central Fires
                    which dotted the length
                         of the central hall

There was much merriment that day

For
    the People held a celebration
        in honor of this New Wisdom

"We have more than we know"
    - - they called it - -

    and they danced quietly
        the beginning of the Spring
            they all searched for in their hearts

And from that day

    The People counted three more
        until the snow outside
            was a little shorter than before . .

And three times three
*   until a young boy came back from the stream*
*   struggling his way through the softening snow*
*   to call out to all the People*
*   the first signs of cracking ice*

And
*   all the young boys rushed outside*
*   to search for new wood*
*   for sharpened stick lances*
And
*   all the young girls toiled patiently once more*
*   over the nets that would soon festoon*
*   the stream-side trees*

For I tell you now
*   this was that very Spring*
*   when the leaves were especially soft . .*
*   and when the Earth herself*
*   seemed eager to split apart*
*   encouraging all the new spring grasses*

And

 when the first shoots of green corn
  appeared through the folds of Earth
   the People celebrated as never before - -
 feet grown slowly stronger
  sounded their thanks on the Earth
   echoed in the constant beating of drums
    which were sacred to this purpose

And

 many voices rang through Elm and Birch
  who, with their bark
   had also enabled this celebration - -

When at last
 the People had, indeed, expressed their joy
  in things growing again
   one among them rose to speak

"You have seen how it is
   my Brothers, my Sisters

You have seen how a lean winter
   may be followed by a winter
      which is leaner yet . .
   And how the summer between
   may be of little benefit

"Let us now resolve
   to learn from this

   "Let no summer pass
      which is full of ripening Corn
         when none is saved
            for the following Winter

   "Let no summer pass
      which is full of ripening Beans
         when none is saved for the Winter
            that follows after that

"Let no summer pass
   that is full of ripening Squash
      when none is saved
         even for the Third Winter

"Let us not again
   peel bark from lodge poles
      for want
         of First Winter preparations

"Let us not again
   See the young among us
      shrink slowly before our eyes
         for want
            of Second Winter preparations

"Let us not again
   chance the well being of the People
      for want
         of Third Winter preparations

"From this day forward . .

    "Let us choose to be a People
      prepared for no less
        than three difficult years

    "Let us choose to be
      a People who survive
        even the Third Winter"

"And from that day to this," my father went on, "The People have always saved from summer's bounty more than One Winter requires - - more even than Two Winters might require - - enough at last for the Third Winter.

"Even in this land of Things Grow in Winter .. even here .. you and I save something for the Third Winter."

And it was so - -

For even though our garden grew throughout the year under the California sun, in the back of our kitchen pantry always lay Corn my father and I had dried .. and Beans and Squash . . . and the cans of tuna fish I also thought appropriate.

"A new friend to join our Three Sacred Sisters," my father chuckled. And the cans of tuna were gathered from our grocery box in much the same manner as we gathered Corn from our garden, then placed with ceremony at the back of the pantry shelf which was sacred to us.

Now you might think that . . living in a land of Winter plenty . . none of these things we kept so carefully would have any other purpose. But I tell you now it was not so.

For the time was such that my father . . who walked the second story beams of houses being built . . found no more such houses to build. And the times were such that our Three Sacred Sisters - - Corn, Beans, and the seeds of Pumpkin - - found their way into the soil of our Winter garden, sustaining life.

And my cans of tuna fish . . one by one . . came down from our pantry shelf to provide our Sunday dinner.

"Better than bark," my father proclaimed and sang from time to time during each such meal a song of thanks for such wisdom.

All but three of those cans were gone before my father found work again. And for those three we had designed a different purpose.

"We give . . and we take from Life," my father said. "If we forget to give . . we have forgotten too much."

And so those three last cans never took their place beside the small wooden box my father had carefully crafted to hold the last three seeds of each kind against any difficult Winter which might follow.

These three last cans we chose to give to others, less fortunate than we, along with some of the new corn. For they also lived within our House, within the larger House of our Great City.

"They need it more than we," he agreed, "for you see, they have no child within their small house with the wisdom to preserve this ocean Brother against a leaner Winter."

"Perhaps they also lack a father who explains such things," I suggested.

"Perhaps they do," he laughed. "And yet, perhaps one day all Earth's children will learn Third Winter wisdom . . and teach themselves how such things may be accomplished wherever they may be. Perhaps tuna fish needs to become one of our Sacred Sisters. Perhaps something quite else may be added. Even in the scarcest land, it seems to me, wisdom and love teach new possibilities . . love for each other . . love for the Earth.

"And perhaps one day we will all learn the value of sharing within the House . . and come to understand how Great that House may be."

I understood my father's words. For a Long House is built in such a manner that we need only add a little to its length in order to include new people.

"It was our thought . . that perhaps one day Earth's children would be wise enough to build so Great a House that its length would reach straight round this Earth and include us all as Brothers."

"As Sisters, too," I reminded.

And my Father smiled.

The Author

Paula Underwood wrote *Winter White and Summer Gold* as a gift for all Earth's children. An oral historian, her lifelong training in an ancient Native American methodology has uniquely prepared her to share these histories with us. In addition to her writing, she is a trainer and consultant whose work in cross-cultural understanding is also based on decades of professional experience in International Communications.

Paula won the Thomas Jefferson Cup for quality writing, and is Executive Director of *The Past is Prologue* Educational Program which was granted "Exemplary Educational Program" status by the U.S. Department of Education. In addition to creating learning experiences for educators and their students, she has developed training programs for corporate executives.

Paula has served as liaison between the Institute of Noetic Sciences and the Worldwide Indigenous Science Network. The Network is designed to help reclaim ancient knowledge, to engender respect for its wisdom, and to encourage a dialogue between Indigenous sciences and Western science. Now she increasingly works with Learning organizations — schools and corporations — as well as an expanded network of Learners.

Paula Underwood was born in Los Angeles and after 35 years in Washington, DC, lives now near San Francisco.

The Artist

Frank Howell, one of America's most highly collected artists, is best known for his intricately-detailed renderings of American Indians. He views these works as universal symbols — as a kind of visual mythology.

Reared and educated in the Midwest, Howell has been painting for over thirty years, and in addition to his acrylics and oils, is well known for his lithographs, monotypes, watercolors, drawings, and sculpture. He has taught on both highschool and college levels, has written several books, and has illustrated many others.

Frank Howell lives and works in Santa Fe, New Mexico, and his work may be seen in galleries there and throughout the United States.